Battle Abbey and Battlefield

Jonathan Coad

Introduction

The battle of Hastings, which took place here on 14 October 1066, was the most famous battle fought on English soil and resulted in the last wholly successful hostile invasion of this country. The triumph of Duke William of Normandy over King Harold marked the end of Anglo-Saxon England, the replacement of its Scandinavian links by new ties with western Europe, and the imposition of a new and more cohesive ruling class. Society became bound by ties of feudal loyalty, leading to a greater concentration of power in royal hands, while the beginnings of the development of common law had consequences that still affect our lives today after nearly 1,000 years.

King William I marked his victory by establishing the great Benedictine abbey of Battle on the northern part of the battlefield. As a result of the king's generous endowments, it became one of the richest monastic houses in England. The abbey flourished for over 400 years until King Henry VIII suppressed the monasteries and disbanded religious communities in the late 1530s. Henry gave Battle Abbey to his friend Sir Anthony Browne who demolished many of the monastic buildings, including the church. He turned the abbot's lodging into a substantial private house, at the centre of an estate created from the former battlefield and abbey land.

In 1721, the estate passed to the Websters, who owned it for most of the following 250 years. During this time, large portions of estate land were sold, and many of the monastic buildings fell into ruin. After the First World War, the house was leased to Battle Abbey School. Despite a terrible fire and a hiatus during the Second World War, when the house was used by the War Office, the school continues to occupy it. Today, the site is in the care of English Heritage, and visitors can explore the famous battlefield and a number of the impressive abbey buildings.

Above: William the Conqueror depicted in a mid-13th-century manuscript. The king holds a model of a church, possibly the one at Battle Abbey

Facing page: The magnificent 13th-century vaulted novices' chamber underneath the south end of the monks' dormitory

The Tour

The history of Battle Abbey falls into three phases. First, the site was a battlefield; on 14 October 1066 the hilltop on which the abbey now stands was crowded with King Harold's English army awaiting battle in an east–west line along the ridge. Across the valley to the south was Duke William's Norman army.

Later, after the battle of Hastings, the hillside was levelled for the abbey buildings. These were laid out on a conventional plan, with an inner court to the south of the abbey church and an outer court to the west.

Finally, after the Suppression in 1538, the abbey became a country estate, and many of the surviving buildings date from this time.

FOLLOWING THE TOUR

In the visitor centre beyond the gatehouse, an exhibition describes the dramatic events of 1066. The tour begins with the battlefield. Visitors follow either the battlefield walk (1 mile) or the shorter terrace route (see page 9). The tour continues around the monastic buildings. The numbers beside the headings highlight key points on the tour and correspond with the numbered plans in the margins.

▮ BATTLEFIELD

The death and violence of the battle of Hastings, fought here on 14 October 1066, have left no visible trace and nor have relics of the battle ever been found. Only the former abbey stands as a near-contemporary memorial to the events that day. The rest of the battlefield now reflects its subsequent use as a park and farmland.

The battlefield path leaves the western end of the terrace and dips through a small copse before emerging onto open sloping ground. Lying south of the main fighting, this area would have seen William's army advancing up the hillside as well as some of the skirmishing as the English later pursued retreating elements of William's forces. Today, the land is grazed much as it was when it formed part of the abbey's great park and later the estate park. However, it is possible to see the slight earthworks of post-medieval field boundaries, and an 18th-century estate map marks this area as a hop garden. The mature trees scattered on the battlefield probably date from the latter part of the 19th century, when the duke and duchess of Cleveland owned the abbey.

Further down the hillside, the path passes a pond before reaching the top of a gorse-covered hillock. This might have been where a number of the English were trapped and killed early in

Left: Looking north across the lower slopes of the battlefield towards the abbey. The two towers on the left are all that remains of the upper levels of the monastic guest range. In the centre, with its cluster of chimneys, is the library wing built by the duke and duchess of Cleveland in 1858. To its right is the south window of the 15th-century abbot's great hall

Facing page: A detail of the south front of the great gatehouse, built, like the rest of the abbey, of local sandstone. The two niches probably once contained statues of saints

The Landscape of the Battlefield

The battlefield remains remarkably intact after nearly 950 years

In nearly 950 years since the Norman Conquest, the site of the battle has remained remarkably intact. The greatest impact on the battlefield was the construction of the abbey buildings where the English army had fought and died. The monks levelled the hilltop for the church and cloister, but made fewer alterations to the ground levels in the outer court. The latter was only levelled in the early 18th century when it was landscaped into a series of formal open spaces divided by lines of trees and fences. In the later 19th century, elaborate gardens were laid out in the cloister and south of the former guest range.

The remainder of the battlefield became part of the abbey's great park, maintained primarily for hunting and exercise. The surrounding woods were managed for timber, and the battlefield was used for growing arable crops, cattle grazing and horse breeding. Fish, an important part of the monastic diet, partly came from ponds that were formed along the valley floor. This mixed use of arable and grazing land continued into the 20th century. However, under the Websters, who owned the abbey during the 18th and 19th centuries, financial difficulties led to the cutting down of most of the park's trees and quarrying of the underlying sandstone. The parkland was restored by the duke and duchess of Cleveland, who bought the Battle estate in 1857, and used for grazing cattle and horses.

Right: This view, looking north towards the abbey, shows the slope of the battlefield, with the buildings on the levelled hilltop

Battle to Hastings road. At the start of the battle, the army would have advanced across the valley to engage the English forces, probably leaving reserves of men, horses and weapons here, to be joined by a growing toll of wounded. The view north to the abbey emphasizes the commanding heights held by the English army.

Unless the autumn of 1066 had been unusually dry, the valley bottom would have been boggy but would have presented little obstacle to either army. The three ponds were added later, probably originally dug as fish ponds for the abbey, perhaps to supplement other fish ponds a little further south at Peppering Eye. Well into the 19th century they helped supply water to drive grinding and mixing machinery in the gunpowder mills lower down the valley. The occasional concrete foundations in the grass on this hillside are relics from when the army was stationed here during the Second World War.

From the site of the Norman lines, the route crosses the valley round the uppermost pond, to the gate just below and to the right of the abbey buildings. We can only speculate as to the events on these lower slopes during the battle. William must have ridden across the field somewhere here to rally his forces early in the battle when the Bretons showed signs of retreating in panic. Here, too, his army probably regrouped and rested between assaults on the English shield wall. In later centuries, this heavy clay land provided pasture for cattle and horses. During and immediately after the Second World War, the country's desperate need for food saw these fields also used for cereal growing.

the battle, when they rashly pursued some of the retreating Breton forces. However, the mound as it now exists was largely formed in the 18th century by debris from stone quarrying, which accounts for the surrounding uneven ground. A century later, the mound was called the 'mountain plantation', and it might have become a viewing point over the estate.

South of the mound, the path passes a large pond dug in the valley floor early in the 19th century. It then emerges on the opposite hillside, generally thought to be where William drew up his forces before the start of the battle. We have little idea of the precise extent and location of his army, but we do know that in the centre were the Normans. To their left, or west, were the Bretons, while the French lay at the eastern end, probably partly on the ridge that now carries the

Above: A scene from the Bayeux Tapestry, possibly showing the hillock where a number of English soldiers were trapped and killed during the battle
Left: An illumination from a 13th-century manuscript showing St Benedict and two monks by a fish pond. The Benedictines were known as the black monks from the colour of their habits

King Harold's Rivals to the English Throne

Harold swore an oath of loyalty to William and promised to support his claim to succeed Edward the Confessor

After the death of King Edward the Confessor (1042–66) in January 1066, King Harold faced two main rivals to his throne: King Harold Hardrada of Norway (1047–66) and Duke William of Normandy. Harold Hardrada ('the ruthless') based his claim to the English throne on a treaty of 1038 made by his father Magnus with Harthacnut, king of England from 1040 to 1042.

Duke William's claim was more complex. Edward the Confessor's mother, Queen Emma (d.1052), was the daughter of Duke Richard I of Normandy (942–96) and the great-aunt of William, making William a distant, though illegitimate, cousin of Edward. There were also more personal links between Edward and William, important in an age when the hereditary principle of succession to the throne was not yet firmly established. During the reigns of King Cnut (d.1035) and his two sons, Edward the Confessor lived his formative years as an exile in the Norman court and in 1051 might have named William as his heir. More importantly, Harold also visited France in 1064 or early 1065. The reasons for this trip are now unknown, but after falling into the hands of Guy, count of Ponthieu, Harold was passed as a hostage to William. According to Norman sources, Harold then swore an oath of loyalty to William, agreeing

to press William's claim to succeed Edward the Confessor to the English throne. This oath was largely used by William to justify his subsequent actions. But, as Harold and his supporters well knew, any oath taken under duress, as was probably the case here, was invalid, would be condemned by the Church and could therefore be ignored.

THE ABBEY

The northern part of the battlefield is overlain by the buildings of the inner court of the monastery, which later became a house. When the abbey church was built in the 1070s, it was sited on the ridge so that the high altar could be placed on the spot where Harold had been killed. The private quarters of the monks round the cloister to the south therefore had to be constructed on a steep slope. The first monastic buildings were almost entirely replaced during the 13th century with the buildings that we see today.

2 TERRACE WALK AND 3 GUEST RANGE

The terrace walk overlooks the southern part of the battlefield. It was largely a creation of the duke and duchess of Cleveland in the later 19th century. At the west end, on the north side, a heavily buttressed wall, infilled window and large blocked doorway are the remains of a monastic barn, possibly of 13th-century date. This stood at the south-west corner of the outer court.

Next to it is the lower storey of the 13th-century monastic guest range, constructed close to the abbot's house to accommodate his more important visitors. After Battle's suppression in 1539, the Browne family, who were given the abbey by King Henry VIII, reconstructed it to form a substantial two-storey guest wing. It was demolished in the middle of the 18th century with the exception of the two western towers and the undercrofts. Surviving illustrations show a substantial range, with crenellated parapets, echoing those of the earlier gatehouse across the outer court. A later doorway from the terrace leads into the eight vaulted medieval undercrofts. Just inside this entrance are the remains of a corner fireplace, suggesting that there might have been a small office for a monastic official here. All these rooms were originally separate from one another and were entered from the northern side, as can be seen by the series of windows and doorways blocked when the level of the outer court was raised in the early 18th century. Originally, these were probably storerooms for the abbey cellarer; during the more neglected periods of the estate in the 18th century they were reputedly used by smugglers to store contraband. The internal linking doorways are modern.

Above: The remains of the monastic guest range with the pair of 16th-century towers. The surviving undercrofts were used as storerooms by the abbey, with the guest quarters on the floors above

Below: One of the earliest known drawings of the abbey, made in about 1700. Prominent in the foreground is the former monastic guest range as rebuilt by Sir Anthony Browne in the mid-16th century

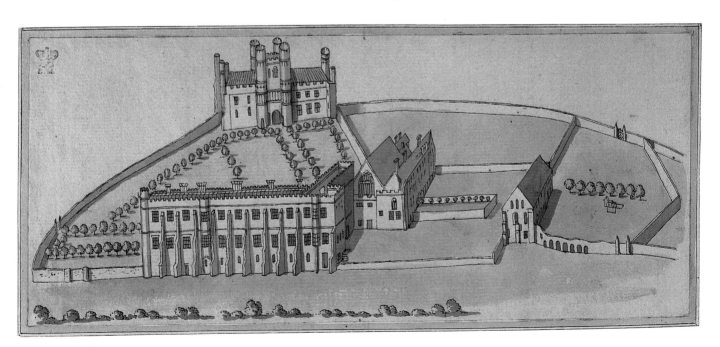

LATRINES

1 Traces of barrel vaults

2 Doorways from dormitory

3 First-floor doorway

4 Doorway to further latrine over drain

5 Channel for main drain

6 Arched south wall

EAST RANGE
4 Latrines

The monastic east range, with its huge dormitory and associated latrines, largely dates from a major rebuilding campaign in the 13th century, when the community improved its living quarters.

The three-storey latrine block projects east from the southern end of the dormitory and was once nearly as tall as the dormitory. Traces of two barrel vaults that supported the second floor and the row of latrines along the south side of the building can still be seen in the dormitory wall. Monks reached the latrines directly from the dormitory by two doorways. Below the remains of the vaults, the larger doorway linked the first floor with the ground floor of the dormitory range, and the smaller doorway linked the dormitory range to a further latrine over the main drain. The ground floor was once a substantial vaulted room with a main entrance, windows, and a fireplace in its north wall. At a later stage, a small room was created at the eastern end. These ground- and first-floor rooms might have been living quarters for the novice monks.

Clean water and drainage were central to monastic planning, where standards of hygiene tended to be higher than in the secular world. Wherever possible, clean running water was channelled through the monastery, first to the kitchen and washing places, and then to the latrines to flush the main drain. Battle Abbey's hilltop site made an adequate supply of running water a particular problem, and the absence of a contained channel beneath the latrines, behind the arches of the south wall, suggests that the drain had to be cleaned out periodically like a cesspit.

Facing page: The east range from the site of the abbey church. The dormitory was on the upper floor

Below: A reconstruction drawing of the latrine range showing the latrines on the second floor

5 Novices' Chamber

The remarkable vaulted ground-floor rooms below the dormitory give an impression of the quality of all the buildings at Battle Abbey before they were ruined. Conventionally, novice monks used the southernmost room beneath the dormitory as a common room, although at Battle there were never many novices. As it is well lit and has the only ground-floor fireplace, this room might also have been used as a day room for writing and work, doubling as the warming room during winter, when a fire was allowed. Originally, the walls were plastered and probably painted with thin red lines to suggest fine masonry. Traces of such decoration survive in some of the window openings of the dormitory above.

The main entrance is on the western side. The remarkable height of the room reflects the need on this hillside to create a level floor for the dormitory above. A single row of columns of Sussex marble carries the vaults. Near the southern end of the east wall are traces of a wall shaft and vaulting from the earlier pre-13th-century building. The southern of the three lancet windows in this wall was restored after 1902 to replicate the original window that had been damaged by the later insertion of a doorway. The narrow stairway in the south-east corner leads to a latrine; the wider doorway once led to the lower part of the latrine block range and may well be a later alteration. In the south wall are the remains of the substantial fireplace; the marks of its hood are clearly visible above the tiled fireback. Smoke escaped through a chimney within a hollow buttress outside. Despite the size of the fireplace, it is unlikely that this room was ever really warm in winter.

6 Passage

The room next to the novices' chamber to the north is decorated with high-quality carved corbels supporting the vaults. Its original use is unknown. To the north is a barrel-vaulted passage (known as the slype). This was the main route between the cloister and the buildings of the monks' infirmary that lay to the east. The infirmary, where sick and infirm monks were cared for, no longer survives above ground. The early 19th-century ice house and dairy now stand on part of this area.

7 Common Room

Immediately north of the slype, and with its main entrance from the cloister, is a further handsome room, lit by a line of five lancet windows in the eastern wall. The builders lavished considerable care here, notably in the double row of Sussex marble columns and the carved stone corbels in the walls that support the vaulting. The location suggests that this room was the monks' common room – the winter chill perhaps being lessened by portable charcoal braziers. The two openings in the north wall are early 20th-century insertions.

8 Inner Parlour

North of the common room are the remains of a narrow, vaulted, rectangular room. This was the inner parlour, one of the few places where monks were allowed essential conversations, silence being the general rule. To discourage dallying and idle gossip, the room was deliberately austere and served partly as a corridor. A doorway at its eastern end once led to the monks' infirmary.

Below: The soaring south end of the east range reflects the difficulty in providing a level floor for the dormitory on the first floor because of the steep slope of the hillside

Facing page: The handsomely vaulted north chamber of the east range was perhaps the monks' common room

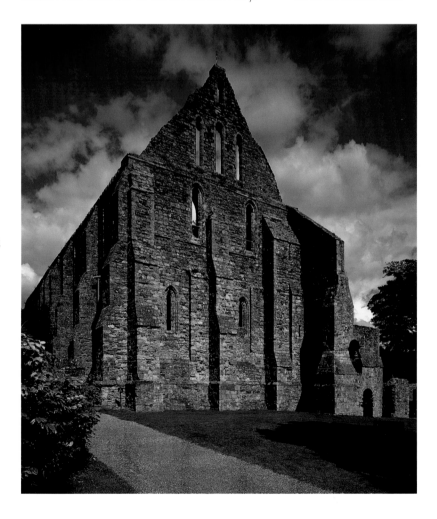

Right: Looking south across the site of the chapter house towards the east range. The dormitory occupied the whole of the upper floor

9 Chapter House

Between the inner parlour and the site of the south transept of the abbey church are the remains of the chapter house. Together with the abbey church, this building was central to the life of the monastic community. The monks met here every day, sitting on benches round the walls, to discuss the business of the community with the abbot or prior and to hear a chapter of the Rule of St Benedict.

The chapter house was an apsidal-ended building. Although the plan remained largely unaltered after its completion in about 1100, excavations between 1978 and 1980 showed that about a century later, before the reconstruction of the rest of the cloister buildings, it was extensively modernised. It was lit by new windows and given a handsome stone wall arcade round the interior. In common with many other chapter houses, some monks of the community were buried here.

10 Dormitory

The vast scale of the monastic dormitory is best appreciated from the area of the chapter house. Lit by a series of lancet windows with shutters in their lower halves, it was second only to the abbey church in size. Originally, this austere unheated room with its high ceiling would have been a large open space. Its white plastered walls were decorated with thin red lines painted to simulate masonry joints, and the beds of the monks were arranged in rows against the walls.

However, the insertion of a small number of fireplaces, probably in the 15th century, suggests that at Battle the monks followed the common later monastic practice of lightly partitioning the dormitory into cubicles, opening off a wide central corridor. A 1501 reference to desks

Dormitory range

Section

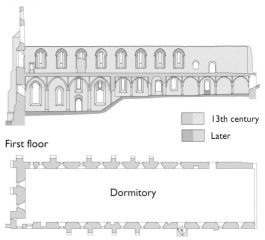

13th century
Later

First floor

Dormitory

Ground floor

Novices' chamber
Common room

Passage

0   15 metres

0   15 yards

N

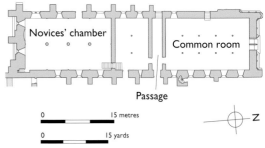

study-bedrooms. The doorway at the north end of the west wall led to an external stair to the cloister; the scars of the steps remain on the wall beneath. It is unlikely that there was direct access connecting the dormitory to the church, so the external stairway was probably also used by the monks on their way to and from night-time services. In the east wall is a further small spiral stair entered from outside the building, perhaps used by the prior on his rounds or for access to maintain the roof. In 1369, the roof was covered in wooden shingles; these had been replaced with tiles by the time of Battle's suppression. The dormitory remained roofed until the end of the 18th century, when the roof collapsed; it was possibly used for a time as a barn and also briefly as stables, approached by an earthen ramp at the north end. The floor was originally tiled, but these floor tiles did not survive the room's use as stables. The earthen ramp was only removed during conservation work by the archaeologist Sir Harold Brakespear in the 1930s.

in the dormitory, and the discovery during the 1980 excavations in the latrine block of a large number of writing instruments and book remnants thrown here at the time of Battle's suppression, further suggest that in its later years the dormitory was converted into a series of

Left: The interior of the dormitory looking north. This painting was made by Samuel Grimm in 1783, shortly before the roof collapsed

Below: The dormitory range from the south-east, painted by Samuel Grimm in 1783. He shows the buildings in a state of disrepair

Right: The west range undercroft dates to the 13th century and was used as a drawing room by the duke and duchess of Cleveland, who bought the abbey in 1857

THE CLOISTER AND WEST RANGE

1. Stub of south wall of refectory
2. Part of a refectory lancet window
3. Remains of 13th-century blind tracery in the refectory
4. Traces of 11th-century Romanesque arcading
5. Cloister walk
6. Door to outer parlour
7. 13th-century tracery
8. 15th-century tracery
9. Site of 13th-century abbot's hall
10. Cloister garden

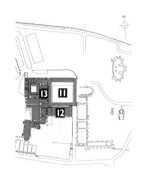

⑪ CLOISTER

The cloister walks, now indicated by gravel paths, linked the principal buildings of the abbey, with the church to the north, the cellarer's range or abbot's house to the west, the refectory to the south and the dormitory to the east. The sunny north walk, in the sheltered lee of the church, was often used by the monks as a scriptorium or writing area for the production of books.

Originally, simple lean-to roofs probably protected the cloister walks. Abbot Walter de Luci (1139–71) had the cloister rebuilt with pavements and columns of local Sussex marble. Further modifications followed, notably the introduction of elaborate tracery and vaulting, remains of which can be seen on the ground floor of the west range. Here, the two bays of blind tracery at the southern end belong to the 13th century and the remaining seven to the north to a further reconstruction in the 15th century. They were pierced with windows after Battle's suppression. Although now a lawn, the centre of the cloister was probably laid out by the monks as a garden.

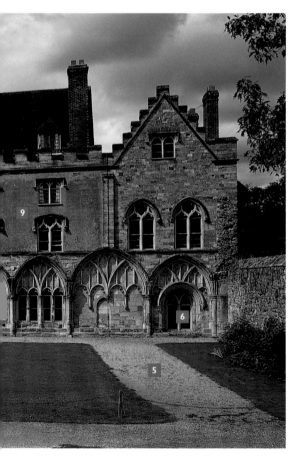

SOUTH RANGE

⑫ Refectory

The monastic refectory or dining room, which formed the south range, was largely rebuilt in the 13th century. It was almost totally demolished after Battle Abbey was suppressed, but its plan was marked out in the grass in the 1930s. The stub of its south wall, with part of a lancet window, can be seen projecting from the west range. Below this, and running along its former west wall, are the remains of the elaborate blind arcade tracery that once decorated the interior of the 13th-century refectory. Behind and a little above this on the west wall is the ghost of the earlier Romanesque arcading from the original late 11th-century building. South of the refectory, and also marked out in the grass, is the plan of the great monastic kitchen, which was demolished between 1683 and 1687.

⑬ WEST RANGE AND ABBOT'S LODGING

In a Benedictine abbey, the west range, situated between the outer court and the cloister, was originally used by the cellarer for the storage of provisions, and as guest accommodation. In the mid-13th century, under Abbot Ralph of Coventry (1235–61), it was converted into a house for the abbot, his household staff and important guests. Mitred abbots of Battle, members of the House of Lords, were powerful men with major landholdings. As such, they would need to be able to entertain distinguished visitors, including monarchs and their retinues, in appropriate accommodation. In effect, the west range became a grand house – a development mirrored at other monasteries and one that was to give it a continuing use after Battle was suppressed, when most of the other monastic buildings were destroyed.

The extensive 13th-century rebuilding retained the outer parlour on the ground floor at the northern end. This provided a link between the cloister and the outer court and was the only place where monks could meet visitors. Its eastern doorway, now filled with a two-light window, is within the northernmost vaulted bay of the west range. In the 13th century, the main accommodation was on the first floor above vaulted undercrofts, with a great hall parallel

Right: A drawing of the interior of the 15th-century abbot's hall in 1783, by Samuel Grimm. The hall was badly damaged in a fire in 1931, and was afterwards restored by the architect Harold Brakespear

Below: The interior of the library in the west range, built by the duke and duchess of Cleveland in the 1850s. The photograph was taken when the estate was put up for sale in 1891

to the cloister and a great chamber projecting west from its south end, with a private chapel for the abbot. In the 15th century a second great hall was added to the west of the refectory, with a new porch created below the abbot's chapel. This formed the nucleus of the post-monastic country house, which remained substantially intact until 1931. In the early 19th century, the Websters altered many of the windows and built a single-storey service wing to the north-west. In the 1850s the Clevelands added a large library wing, designed by Henry Clutton, to the south-west. Much of the west range was rebuilt internally after a severe fire caused extensive damage in 1931. The west range is now occupied by Battle Abbey School and the restored 15th-century great hall and 19th-century library, where the Webster family portraits are hung, can be visited during the school's summer holidays.

▐ ABBEY CHURCH

North of the chapter house, a sandstone plaque in the ground marks the spot where Harold was killed in the early evening of 14 October 1066.

Left: A reconstruction of the east end of the abbey church after modernization and enlargement in the 13th century. The crypt can be seen below the east end of the church

The high altar of the abbey church was later placed here on the express command of William the Conqueror, the building overlying the scene of the fiercest fighting of the battle of Hastings.

Destruction of the church immediately after the suppression of the abbey in 1539 was thorough, and little remains to be seen. Investigation of the site in the 1930s and more recently, however, has enabled a plan of the church to be reconstructed with some accuracy. The original church, begun in about 1071 and completed in 1094, was some 69m (225ft) long. It was an aisled building, with a nave of seven bays and apsidal chapels off the north and south transepts. East of the crossing was a short apsidal presbytery with an ambulatory beyond, leading to three further apsidal chapels. The plan of this east end is marked on the ground. In size and layout, the church reflected contemporary buildings in Normandy and the Loire valley – the location of Marmoutier Abbey, home of the first monks who were brought to England to found Battle Abbey (see page 32). Although modest in scale compared with immediate successors such

as St Augustine's, Canterbury, or Bury St Edmunds Abbey, Battle was probably the first church in England to combine an eastern apse, an ambulatory and radiating chapels. The lower courses of the south aisle wall and a stub of wall with a wall shaft and column capital projecting slightly from the north end of the west range are all that remain of the abbey church.

In the second half of the 13th century, the eastern end of the church, including the monks' choir, was enlarged and modernized following the latest architectural fashion. The original east end was demolished and replaced with a new seven-bay choir 46m (152ft) long, with five radiating chapels – a design derived from King Henry III's rebuilding of Westminster Abbey between 1246 and 1259. The sloping site allowed space for a vaulted crypt with a further three chapels. This rebuilding doubled the number of altars in the church, important to a community where the majority of the monks were ordained priests. The crypt, which was excavated in 1817, is the only part of this work to survive.

15 DAIRY AND ICE HOUSE

To the south-east of the church and partly overlooking the 19th-century walled kitchen garden, stands an octagonal thatched dairy next to an underground ice house. Both are rare survivals. They were built by Sir Godfrey Vassall Webster, probably in about 1818. Ice houses were introduced into England in the late 17th century to store ice harvested from ponds in winter for culinary use throughout the following summer. They remained popular until the introduction of refrigerators in the late 19th century. Small dairies separate from the main house became fashionable in the 18th century. Many owners favoured buildings in a classical style; Sir Godfrey, no doubt influenced by the abbey, chose Gothic. After falling into ruin, the dairy was restored in 1991; adjoining it are the remains of the scullery where utensils were cleaned.

16 PRECINCT WALL

North of the abbey church is the best-preserved length of precinct wall, completed under Abbot Ralph (1107–24). Originally, this would have surrounded the abbey to preserve its privacy and as protection from robbers. The stretch leading to the great gatehouse, alongside the camellia walk planted by the duchess of Cleveland, is unusual for a monastery in having a wall-walk for defensive purposes. This is probably contemporary with the rebuilding of the gatehouse at the start of the Hundred Years War in the 1330s.

17 COURTHOUSE

The courthouse, where visitors now enter the site, was built in the mid-16th century and restored in the 1990s after standing roofless for many years. It replaced a medieval building, probably used by the abbey's almoner, the man responsible for dispensing charity to the poor and sick. This almonry, whose end wall survives as the east wall of the courthouse, replaced a still earlier building. A remnant of this earlier building survives at the north-east corner of the courthouse, with an early 12th-century wall shaft and carved capital on its north face. This is best seen from the precinct wall-walk.

Above: The exterior of the great gatehouse with the courthouse on the left, in a painting by Samuel Grimm of 1783
Left: Inside the thatched dairy, restored in 1991. The modern coloured glass and perforated zinc screens, which keep out birds and insects, are based on original fragments found on site

Facing page: The precinct wall on the north side of the abbey. The parish church of St Mary can be seen beyond

Right: The great gatehouse,
with the courthouse on
the right, seen from within
the former outer court
of the abbey

Right: The great gatehouse, with the courthouse on the right, seen from within the former outer court of the abbey

18 GREAT GATEHOUSE

The great gatehouse that still dominates the town of Battle was begun in 1338 to replace an earlier one. It remains one of the finest in England, constructed not just to provide a magnificent

Gatehouse and courthouse

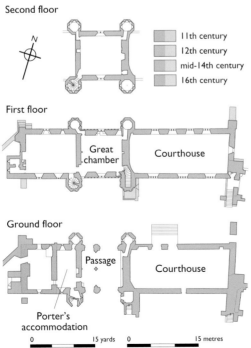

Second floor

11th century
12th century
mid-14th century
16th century

First floor

Great chamber
Courthouse

Ground floor

Passage
Courthouse

Porter's accommodation

0   15 yards   0   15 metres

entrance, but also to increase security. All traffic to the abbey had to pass through it, carts and riders using the larger passageway and pedestrians the smaller one. The narrow doorway in the west wall of the pedestrian passage led to the porter's accommodation; adjacent to this is a blocked window for the porter.

The scale of the great gatehouse and the wealth of its decorative stonework were designed to reflect the power and importance of the abbey. The corner turrets contain stairs to the two upper floors and the roof. Although the crenellations and arrow slits, and the adjacent wall-walk, emphasize the defensive nature of the gatehouse and precinct wall, these were not serious fortifications capable of withstanding prolonged assault or siege. They could have provided short-term resistance, either to the small-scale French raids that plagued coastal areas during the Hundred Years War, or to riotous locals and bands of robbers.

Both upper floors of the gatehouse formed substantial private apartments for the use of senior abbey officials or visitors. Another grand apartment was created on the first floor of the contemporary west range, above the porter's accommodation. This west range incorporates parts of the original late 11th-century gatehouse, including two small, round-headed windows in the north wall. The original entrance roadway lay a little to the west of the present gate-passages.

The slightly later small porch on the south-east turret leads to a vaulted stair. Halfway up the stair are the grooves for a portcullis and in the vault overhead are two murder-holes for defendants to rain missiles on assailants on the stairs. The stair opens into the great chamber over the gate-passage; immediately on the left is a doorway leading to the portcullis room. The sophisticated defences for the great chamber might reflect its possible use by the abbey steward, who needed to protect his legal records and the money from rents and sales of abbey produce.

In the west wall of the great chamber is a modern copy of a magnificent medieval fire hood, fragments of which were found reused as blocking material in the fireplace during conservation work in 1988. Originally, this chamber would have been simply furnished, probably with a bed, a table, a chest and some benches and chairs near the fire.

In the south-west corner, a modern doorway allows access to a similarly grand chamber in the west range. This too was once self-contained and was approached by the spiral stair in the south-west turret. In the west wall is a handsome stone fireplace. To its right is a blocked Norman window from the earlier gatehouse and on its left is a cupboard. The floor and ceiling were reinstated in the late 1980s in their 14th-century positions. Although now one room, it is possible that the north-eastern part may have been partitioned off as a separate bedchamber, lit by the single-light window in the north wall. In the opposite corner a narrow doorway leads to a two-cell latrine.

We can only speculate as to who used these grand lodgings. They were probably for senior abbey officials – the beadle, collector of the abbey rents, or the steward. By the 1330s, monks responsible for legal aspects of the community's life were being replaced by stewards starting their careers in administration or law, drawn from the gentry of Kent or Sussex. For such men, the gatehouse apartments would have provided suitable accommodation and office space, well-sited overlooking the town and the outer court.

Below: A watercolour of the great gatehouse in 1792 by Michael Angelo Rooker (1746–1801). The upper floors were then used for storage and doors had replaced windows

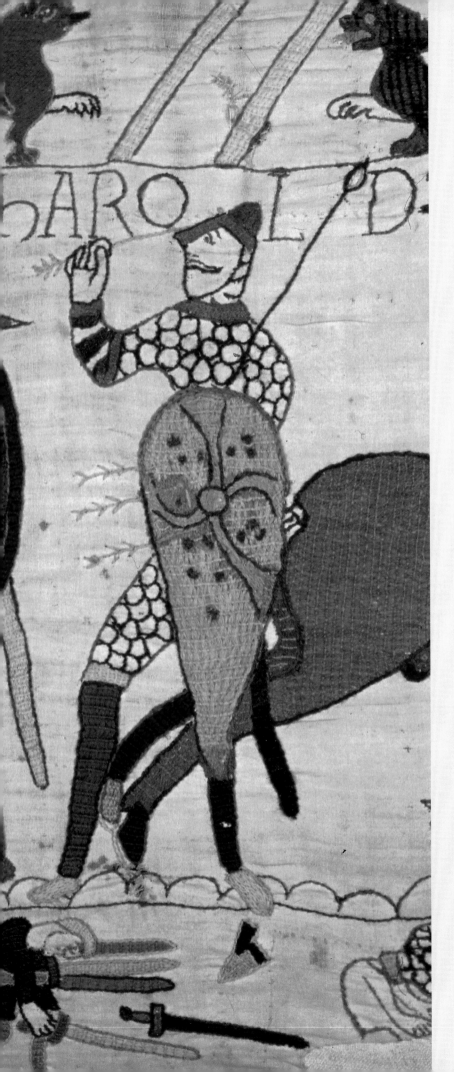

History

The site of Battle Abbey was an empty hillside until 14 October 1066, when it became the location of one of the most important events in English history – the battle of Hastings. Following the defeat of the English and the death of King Harold, William the Conqueror founded the abbey to commemorate his victory and as penance for the bloodshed. Benedictine monks lived here until the abbey was suppressed, and the buildings were given to a courtier and friend of King Henry VIII. The abbey was run as a private estate until the 20th century. Today, after nearly 950 years, the site remains a potent symbol of one of the most significant dates in English history.

READING THE HISTORY

This section describes the history of the battle of Hastings, the foundation of the abbey, and its later history as a private country residence. There are features on the Bayeux Tapestry and historical sources for the battle (page 31), Domesday Book (page 32), the monks' day (page 39) and an account of the devastating fire of 1931 (page 47).

1066 – BEFORE THE BATTLE

The momentous events of 1066 and their consequences stemmed from the death on 4 January that year of King Edward the Confessor. Edward had died childless, leaving no direct heir to the throne. England in 1066 was a prosperous agricultural land with an extensive system of communal strongholds, known as burghs, protecting its citizens from raids. It had a well-equipped and semi-professional army – the fyrd – that supported the king's own retainers known as housecarls. It also had a powerful navy to guard its coasts and to counter raids from Scandinavia and elsewhere. Such assets made the English throne a glittering prize. In 1066 there were three main contenders for the kingdom, all with varying degrees of legitimacy to justify their claims: Earl Harold of Wessex, King Harold Hardrada in Norway, and Duke William of Normandy. In his dying days, the king and his advisors faced an agonizing decision. All knew that Edward's choice of successor would almost certainly be challenged by his rivals, and that invasion or civil war threatened the country.

The best hope was for a quick succession and a strong king who could command support in the country. This ruled out Edward's nearest relation, his great-nephew Edgar Aethling, then in his early teens. Edward's eventual choice of Earl Harold of Wessex was both pragmatic and inevitable. Although Harold had no royal blood, his sister was

married to the king; more importantly, Harold was the most powerful noble in the country and head of the royal army. The day after Edward's death, Harold was consecrated king in Westminster Abbey. In his brief reign he showed himself to be an able administrator and an outstanding commander.

Harold's first challenge came in May 1066 when his brother Tostig, who was in exile in Flanders, landed with forces in eastern England. This was more of a raid than a serious invasion and was soundly beaten by Earl Edwin of Mercia. For the rest of the summer, Harold kept his main forces on the Isle of Wight, with further troops along the south coast. The English fleet stood watch in the Channel; both Hardrada and William were known to be assembling ships and men.

Top: Men defending a fort in an English drawing of about AD 1000. Although illustrating a biblical story, it might represent a burgh
Above: A silver penny minted in the reign of King Harold
Left: The coronation of Harold from the Bayeux Tapestry. On the left Harold is given the crown, and on the right he sits on his throne

Facing page: The scene in the Bayeux Tapestry believed to show Harold fatally wounded with an arrow through an eye

By early September, Harold might have felt that the approach of autumn gales would deter overseas invasions until the spring, and as the Anglo-Saxon Chronicle recorded, 'When the festival of the Nativity of St Mary [8 September] came, the men's provisions had run out, and no one could keep them there any longer: they were therefore given permission to return home.' A day or so later, Harold Hardrada's invading forces suddenly appeared off the north-east coast, sailing up the River Ouse to land near York on about 16 September.

King Harold reacted with astonishing speed. Assembling his army, he moved swiftly north and in a great and decisive battle at Stamford Bridge on Monday 25 September surprised and defeated the Norwegians, killing Hardrada. Reputedly, over 300 ships had transported Hardrada's army to England; 25 sufficed to carry home the survivors. A day or so later, favourable winds allowed William and his forces to set sail for England from St Valéry at the mouth of the River Somme. By that time, William must have known that Harold had disbanded his army in the south and that Hardrada's forces were menacing the north. More crucially, knowledge that the English fleet had retired, battered by gales, to London, gave William the confidence to put to sea. Unlike the English and Scandinavians, the Normans lacked experience of naval warfare and William's ships, many laden with cavalry, would have been

particularly vulnerable to attack. After an overnight crossing, the Norman forces landed unopposed at Pevensey. A few days later, after constructing a timber and earthwork castle in part of the old Roman fort there, William moved his forces to Hastings.

Tradition states that Harold was still at York when he learnt of William's landing. Gathering together the nucleus of his tired but victorious army, he returned the 190 miles to London in a series of forced rides. Pausing briefly to gather fresh troops, he then set out for the Sussex coast. Perhaps if he had waited longer, he could

have amassed a larger army made up of more experienced men, and the outcome of the battle might have been different. But the king probably hoped to repeat the tactic of surprise that had been so effective at Stamford Bridge, and might also have hoped to prevent his family's lands in Sussex being laid waste by the invaders.

THE OPPOSING ARMIES

There are no precise figures, but it is thought that each of the rival armies probably numbered between 5,000 and 7,000 men. By the standards of the day, these were substantial forces. As the Bayeux Tapestry shows, each was remarkably similar in appearance and equipment. Horses, helmets, mail armour, shields, swords and bows were common to both armies. The Normans used crossbows, probably for the first time in England, and with great success on the dense ranks of the English. In contrast there was a shortage of English archers, perhaps a result of the speed of Harold's advance to Sussex, as bowmen probably travelled on foot. The most striking difference between the two armies was the Norman use of cavalry and the English reliance upon foot soldiers, differences stemming from their divergent military tactics. English armies had long used horses for getting around, but on the battlefield, like the Celts and Vikings, they dismounted and fought on foot. The core of

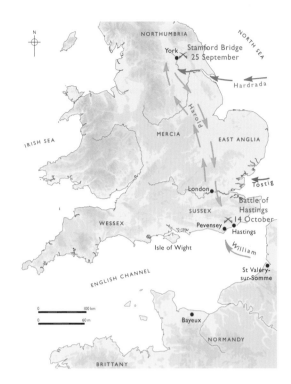

Harold's army was the housecarls, perhaps the finest infantry in Europe, armed with their terrible two-handed battleaxes. In contrast, the backbone of William's forces was his cavalry, perhaps numbering some 2,000–3,000 knights and esquires. When the Viking ancestors of the Normans had settled in Normandy in 911, they had adopted the mounted combat style of the Franks. At the battle of Hastings, these different military cultures met head-on.

Above: A map of England and Normandy showing the locations of the principal events of 1066

Below: The Bayeux Tapestry shows the Norman fleet setting sail for England in late September 1066. The ships are heavily laden with men and horses for the knights

THE BATTLE OF HASTINGS, 14 OCTOBER 1066

All accounts of the battle of Hastings rely on two main sources: the Bayeux Tapestry and the chronicler William of Poitiers (c.1020–90). Although both tell the story from the Norman viewpoint, justifying William's claim to the English throne, they provide far more information than we have for any other medieval battle, although crucial details are still unclear. We know that Harold lost the element of surprise when William learnt of his approach the day before the battle, and moved his own forces 7 miles inland from Hastings to the vicinity of Telham Hill. By that evening the two armies were encamped within sight of each other.

Soon after dawn on 14 October, Harold arranged his forces along the ridge now occupied by the buildings of Battle Abbey. The English line probably stretched for almost half a mile, with the elite housecarls grouped round Harold, his two brothers Gyrth and Loefwine, and the other nobles. The English formed a 'shield wall' on the hilltop. This formation was considered almost impervious to cavalry, but it was cramped and left little room for manoeuvre. William of Poitiers recorded that the soldiers were so close together, that 'the dead could scarcely fall and the wounded could not remove themselves from the action'.

William ranged his army to the south, initially on the far hillside above the marshy valley bottom. His Norman troops were in the centre, probably with Bretons to the west and French to the east. These forces were in three ranks, with the archers in front, then the infantry, some armoured, and behind them the heavy cavalry of knights and esquires.

At about 9am trumpets signalled battle. Then, as now, the landscape must have been sufficiently open to allow the two armies to manoeuvre. The slopes were probably scrubby grazing land, the ridge occupied by the English army backed by the forests of the High Weald. To win, the English needed to stand behind their shield wall, allow the Normans to be decimated in repeated assaults and then sweep forward to defeat the invaders. In contrast, the Normans had to climb the slope to within bowshot of the English – about a couple of hundred metres at most – then fracture the English line with archers and infantry so that the cavalry could ride through and finish off the broken remnants.

Above: The modern memorial window commemorating the battle of Hastings in St Mary's church, Battle
Below: The Norman cavalry advance across the battlefield, in a scene from the Bayeux Tapestry

Facing page: Sunrise over the battlefield, a scene little changed for over 900 years

Right: Norman knights on horseback attempt to break the Saxon shield wall, in this scene from the Bayeux Tapestry

Below: The Bayeux Tapestry shows William raising his helmet to show himself to his army, quelling panic following a rumour that he had been killed

Facing page: William I seated on his throne, as depicted in the late 12th-century Battle Chronicle, written by the monks at Battle Abbey

William of Poitiers recorded, 'It was a strange kind of battle, one side attacking with all mobility, the other withstanding, as though rooted to the soil.' At a time when such contests were frequently decided within an hour, victory at Hastings was not certain until dusk, some nine hours after the fighting began – an indication of just how evenly matched and led the two armies were.

The first Norman attack, using archers, infantry and cavalry, was repulsed, the English battleaxes cleaving the Norman shields and armour. As William's forces regrouped, the Bretons began to retreat and to flee, believing a rumour that the duke was dead. To stop panic spreading, William rode out in front of his troops with his helmet raised, shouting to them so that they could see he was alive and in command. Rallying his men, he led a successful counter-charge and cut down those English forces who had pursued the fleeing Bretons. The immediate crisis had passed.

For the rest of the day, the Normans repeated their assaults on the English line, at least twice pretending to flee to encourage the English to break ranks and pursue them. They were partly successful, but the line held. We can only imagine the grim scene: the wounded, dying and dead men and horses – Duke William apparently had three horses killed beneath him – scattered on a hillside slippery with blood and littered with bodies, arrows and discarded and broken weapons; the increasing tiredness, hunger and fear of the surviving combatants; the commanders such as Eustace of Boulogne and Odo, the fighting bishop of Bayeux, shouting to rally their exhausted forces. With the autumn daylight fading, the Normans made one final effort to take the ridge. By that time, Harold's two brothers and other English commanders were almost certainly dead. During the final assault, the king himself was killed. He was probably fatally wounded by an arrow that pierced his brain through an eye, and then hacked to death as he fell to the ground. Leaderless, and lacking hope, the English forces

The Bayeux Tapestry

finally gave way and fled. William of Poitiers wrote that, 'the Normans, though strangers to the district, pursued them relentlessly, slashing their guilty backs and putting the last touches to the victory. Even the hooves of the horses inflicted punishment on the dead as they galloped over their bodies.'

AFTER THE BATTLE

On 25 December 1066, William was crowned king in Westminster Abbey. Although the battle of Hastings had proved decisive, resistance to the Normans continued. Rebellions in the West Country, the Welsh Marches, the Midlands, the North, and East Anglia were not finally suppressed until 1071. In suppressing these revolts, William could be merciless: his 'harrying of the North' in 1069 and 1070 left large areas of countryside devastated, with cattle, crops and houses destroyed and the inhabitants dead or forced to flee.

To strengthen his legitimacy as king, William was crowned by papal legates at a council at Easter 1070. He followed this with sweeping ecclesiastical and legal reforms, and the wholesale replacement of Anglo-Saxon bishops and abbots by Normans. The English nobility was almost totally displaced and its lands given to William's followers. Everyone was now bound by new feudal ties of loyalty and service to the king. A great building campaign of churches, cathedrals and castles gradually transformed the appearance of much of the country and emphasized Norman authority.

An unusually large number of nearly contemporary sources give us detailed information about the battle of Hastings. William of Poitiers, a Norman soldier, and later William's chaplain, compiled *The Deeds of William, Duke of the Normans and King of England* in about 1071. Although he did not fight at Battle, he clearly knew those who had. William of Jumièges, also a Norman, wrote his *Deeds of the Dukes of the Normans* in about 1070. English sources include versions of the Anglo-Saxon Chronicle, a compilation of contemporary events recorded in different monasteries, and Florence of Worcester's *Chronicle of Chronicles*, compiled about 1118.

In addition to these literary accounts, the battle is brought alive and given an immediacy unique among medieval conflicts by the Bayeux Tapestry. This tells the story of the events largely, but not exclusively, from the Norman perspective from 1064 to the end of the battle, in a sequence of pictorial scenes. It was embroidered in coloured wools on a linen strip some 70m (230ft) long by 50cm (20in) high. The eight sections of the tapestry are of varying lengths, and seem to have been embroidered separately, perhaps in different workshops or by different teams, and then joined together. The final piece is damaged and its end is missing.

It is thought that the tapestry was made shortly after the conquest for Bishop Odo of Bayeux, who features prominently in it and was the half-brother of William. The earliest record of the tapestry is at Bayeux cathedral in 1476, by which time a custom was apparently established to display it each year in the nave. Originally it might have been made for the hall of the bishop's palace.

The similarities between the tapestry and late Saxon manuscript illumination suggest that it might have been embroidered in England, very possibly at Canterbury, then famed for its illuminated manuscripts as well as being the centre of Odo's Kentish estates.

> The battle is brought alive and given an immediacy unique among medieval conflicts by the Bayeux Tapestry

Below: Bishop Odo, who is thought to have commissioned the tapestry, as he appears in it

Domesday Book

'There was not one ox, nor one cow, nor one pig which escaped notice'

Nothing demonstrates the organizational genius of William I better than the compilation of the great Domesday survey. The Anglo-Saxon Chronicle explains what happened:

'The king had important deliberations and exhaustive discussions … about this land, how it was peopled and what sort of men. Then he sent his men all over England … to ascertain how many hundreds of "hides" of land there were in each shire, and how much land and livestock the king himself owned in the country. He also had it recorded … what or how much each man who was a landholder here in England had in land or in livestock, and how much money it was worth. So very thoroughly did he have the inquiry carried out that there was not … one ox, nor one cow, nor one pig which escaped notice.'

This whole survey was apparently completed within a year, with the final compilation and writing-up thought to be mostly the work of just one scribe. No other European ruler for centuries afterwards had so much information about his subjects. The English regarded it with understandable suspicion, naming it Domesday Book – the account compiled on the day of judgement at the end of the world.

Among other information, the survey lists landowners and land values in 1066 and in 1086. Some lands had fallen in value, and are described as being 'wasted', indicating the extent of William's destruction of the country.

THE FOUNDATION OF BATTLE ABBEY

Early tradition recorded that just before the battle of Hastings, Duke William made a vow to establish a monastery on the site of the battle if God granted him victory. This story however only appears for the first time in a forged charter of 1154. It is more probable that William's vow was the result of penances imposed by the papal legates in 1070. Like a great war memorial, the foundation of Battle Abbey could be seen to honour the dead as well as to be a public act of atonement by the king for the bloodshed of the Conquest. In addition, such a grandiose project fitted the Normans' intention of constructing highly visible buildings that represented their power and authority and emphasized the permanency of the Conquest. Situating an abbey on the battlefield would also attract settlers to a comparatively empty stretch of country that had only recently proved to be a good invasion route. In naming it Battle Abbey, the Normans demonstrated their self-confidence and a degree of arrogance.

Four monks from the Benedictine abbey of Marmoutier on the Loire came from France to form the nucleus of the new community. The 12th-century *Chronicle of Battle Abbey* reports that William wished the abbey to be built on the scene of the fiercest fighting, its high altar on the spot where Harold had been killed. This gave the monks a major problem, for a monastery needed a spacious level site and a good supply of running water. The battlefield as a whole was highly unsuitable. The valley bottom was swampy, and

Below: The compiling of Domesday Book resulted in an exhaustive survey of livestock. Battle Abbey itself relied heavily on produce from its own estates. This 11th-century manuscript shows pigs grazing in an orchard

the slope of the hill and the narrow ridge caused serious construction difficulties, while the porous sandstone bedrock lacked a water supply. Faced with these problems, the monks began to build on a more favourable site to the west, but were forced to stop what they were doing when the king heard about it. Commanding them to obey his original instructions, he reputedly promised that, 'If God spare my life I will so amply provide for this place that wine shall be more abundant here than water is at any other great abbey.'

King William I envisaged an initial community of 60 monks at Battle Abbey, rising to an eventual total of 140. All construction costs were to be met from the king's treasury. For the first few years, the monks lived in temporary timber buildings while the hilltop site was levelled and extended, and craftsmen and labourers worked on the church. By 1076, the choir was sufficiently complete to be consecrated and brought into use. In February 1094, 18 years later, the finished church was consecrated in the presence of King William II (1087–1100), Anselm, the new archbishop of Canterbury (1093–1109), seven other bishops and a throng of nobles and courtiers. Construction then focused on the buildings of the cloister and outer court.

When William I died in 1087 he secured the future of the abbey with generous gifts and endowments. The most important of these was the *leuga*, all land within a league or 1½ miles from the high altar of the abbey church. Within this area the abbey had widespread freedom from secular authorities, and the abbot enjoyed supreme jurisdiction over land and men. Other gifts from the king included a royal estate and a manor, as well as lands and churches. Some of William's closest followers also made gifts, and when William died, Battle Abbey had become the 15th richest religious house in England.

Left: A reconstruction of how the interior of the abbey church might have looked soon after its consecration in 1094, looking east towards the choir

Facing page, top: The seal of Battle Abbey showing the 11th-century west front of the abbey church. The seal shows two eastern towers, as well as those of the west front and crossing

Above: A rare 12-century fragment of an ivory cross, forming the top of an ecclesiastical staff, found during excavations at Battle Abbey

Below: A manuscript illustration showing animals in stables. Improved farming methods increased the abbey's income in the 13th century

Facing page: Battle Abbey looking north-east. In the centre is the abbot's lodging. These buildings survived the destruction of the abbey in 1539, becoming the heart of the later house

YEARS OF UNCERTAINTY

In the first 150 years at Battle, the community struggled to maintain the valuable exemption from episcopal control granted to them by William the Conqueror. During the reigns of the first two Norman kings, this did not present a problem, for both took a close interest in the abbey. The task was to sustain this freedom in the long term.

In 1147 Bishop Hilary of Chichester (1147–69), in whose diocese the abbey lay, challenged Battle Abbey's claim to exemption, and excommunicated Battle's abbot, Walter de Luci (1139–71). The abbot appealed to the king, and this row dragged on for ten years. The forged charter detailing William the Conqueror's alleged vow to found the abbey before the battle of Hastings was made at this time to support the abbey's cause. Eventually, Bishop Hilary appealed to the Pope, and in May 1157, both abbot and bishop were summoned to the king's court at Westminster to put their cases to King Henry II (1154–89). Although Henry judged in favour of Battle Abbey, it was not the end of the matter.

After the death of Walter de Luci in June 1171, Henry II, who had no real interest in Battle Abbey, gave Richard de Luci, Walter's brother, control of the abbey for four years. During this time no abbot was appointed and the Luci family enjoyed its surplus income. Eventually, in 1211, the monks paid the substantial sum of 1,500 marks to

King John (1199–1216) to confirm the abbey's liberties and to allow them to be free to elect their own abbots. This marked the end of the royal link with Battle Abbey.

However, the quarrel was not finally settled until the 1230s when Ralph Neville, bishop of Chichester (1224–44) and chancellor of England, appealed to Rome for a ruling. A lasting compromise was reached, preserving enough of the abbey's privileges to recognize its special status, while allowing the bishop to exercise control should anything be found amiss. This was the start of a long and largely harmonious relationship between the two.

YEARS OF PROSPERITY

For Battle Abbey, the 13th century was a time of rising prosperity. In part, this was due to the growth of the town of Battle, but mostly it reflects general changes in farming practices. Wool and wheat could be sold profitably on the open market, encouraging landowners such as the abbots of Battle to manage their estates more efficiently. Under Abbot Ralph of Coventry (1235–61) and Abbot John of Whatlington (abbey steward 1290, abbot 1308–11) in particular, nearby farm tenants were bought out and their land managed directly. Additional land was purchased and the abbey is known to have possessed a copy of Walter of Henley's tract on improved farming methods. Both the introduction of crop rotation, which reduced the need to allow land to lie fallow, and the stall-feeding of animals, which enabled manure to be collected and spread more evenly on fields, helped to increase crop yields.

In the town there was a similar policy of buying out tenants and leasing properties at improved rents. The result of this rising income can be seen today in the surviving abbey buildings. By the start of the 13th century, the original buildings probably seemed old-fashioned and cramped. Over the next 100 years, almost all those round the cloister were completely rebuilt. Most spectacularly, the abbey church was enlarged and extended eastwards in the latest architectural style, modelled on Henry III's great mid-13th-century rebuilding of Westminster Abbey, which would have been admired by abbots of Battle attending the king's court.

LIFE IN THE ABBEY

As at other Benedictine houses, Battle monks lived an enclosed life within the abbey, which was laid out to the standard Benedictine plan, with its buildings arranged round an inner and an outer court and enclosed by a precinct wall.

In the outer court were workshops and blacksmiths' forges, a mason's yard for building maintenance, barns for grain and hay, storehouses, stables and cart sheds, wood for fuel, and offices and accommodation for some of the more important abbey officials such as the steward. Here too, local traders and craftsmen came seeking orders and delivering goods to the abbey cellarer. As the town grew outside the abbey, its high street focused naturally on the great gatehouse.

The buildings of the outer court were probably ranged along the northern, western and southern sides of the precinct walls, where a few still remain. On the eastern side stands the west range of the cloister. Initially, this west range was the preserve of the cellarer, the monk in charge of the community's food and drink. Here he had easy contact with estate staff and suppliers. As with so many monasteries, the range was later converted into the abbot's house.

The inner court was the private heart of the monastery where the monks lived. Dominating this was the abbey church dedicated to St Martin of Tours. Initially, the townspeople of Battle worshipped here, but according to the *Chronicle of Battle Abbey*, 'it was not long before there arose thence causes of disquiet to the monks … Therefore by common agreement they had erected a chapel outside the walls'. This chapel,

rebuilt and extended, is the present parish church of St Mary. South of the abbey church lay the cloister, which linked the church and surrounding buildings. On the eastern side of the cloister lay the chapter house and the dormitory with the buildings of the infirmary beyond. To the south was the refectory or communal dining room; beyond this and separated as a fire precaution stood the great kitchen. Virtually no traces survive of these first monastic buildings; all were largely rebuilt and extended in the 13th century.

We do not know if there were ever as many as the 140 monks intended by William the Conqueror. Later surviving records show a much smaller community. The Black Death of 1348–9 reduced the number of monks from 52 to 34 by 1352. The size of the community apparently remained fairly constant during the 15th century.

The strict daily Benedictine timetable, or *horarium,* regulated the lives of the monks. The timing of services was governed by the seasons and further varied by church festivals and fast days. The monks' rigorous routine was only possible with a sustaining diet. The cellarer's accounts, which survive from 1275 to 1513, show us that the community enjoyed a variety of foods. Outside Lent and periods of fasting, Benedictine monks after 1300 were allowed meat, mainly beef, mutton and pork, for three main meals each week, although the accounts occasionally mention swans, geese, herons and hares. At the other four main meals, fish or eggs were served. Dried, salted or pickled herrings were the staple fish,

Left: An abbey cellarer with a bunch of keys tastes wine, in an illustration from a 13th-century manuscript
Below: *A scene from a 15th-century manuscript showing monks dining in their refectory, served by domestic staff*

Facing page: The great gatehouse rebuilt in 1338, was a symbol of the wealth and power of the abbey

although cod and mackerel bought from Hastings fishermen were also eaten in significant amounts. Freshwater fish came from the abbey's own fish ponds. Bread was always provided, and vegetables came either from the cellarer's garden or the kitchen garden. Broad beans and peas were grown on the abbey estates from the 13th century and oysters and mussels were introduced in the 15th century. Beer was the everyday drink, although cider and wines were also consumed.

On occasion, the monks' routine was varied by contact with the outside world. The abbot of Battle was the equal of a great land-owning nobleman and until 1366, abbots maintained their own household retainers, necessary when providing accommodation for the king and other nobles on their journeys through the area. The abbot was also frequently summoned to take part in the king's court, and the abbey had lodgings in Winchester and London. These were useful when visits were protracted, such as when Abbot Walter de Luci had to stay in London from November 1154 to Lent 1155. The abbot and prior made regular tours of inspection of the abbey's outlying churches and estates elsewhere in England. After the foundation of the Benedictines' own college at Oxford in the last years of the 13th century, some of the Battle monks were able to benefit from a university education. By the end of the 14th century, Battle sent one or two monks at a time to the university, and no doubt their studies enriched the intellectual and religious life of the community. Monks were occasionally allowed on individual pilgrimages; in the years before the abbey's suppression, at least one went as far as Rome.

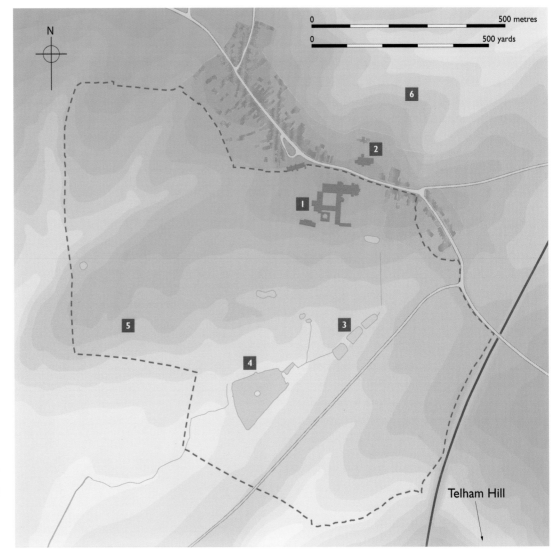

KEY TO BATTLE ABBEY LANDSCAPE

1 Battle Abbey

2 St Mary's church

3 Medieval fish ponds

4 19th-century pond

5 Abbey's great park

6 Abbey's little park

- - - Approximate area of batttle of Hastings battlefield

▨▨▨ Extent of the medieval town of Battle

The abbot and monks could also enjoy the abbey's local lands. Just north-east of the town of Battle was the little park, and immediately south of the abbey buildings was the great park, overlying much of the site of the battle of Hastings. The abbey's manor of Alciston on the Sussex Downs was a favourite resort of successive abbots, and in the 14th century, abbots enjoyed riding and hawking in the marshes of the Pevensey Levels near their manor of Barnhorn. Most of the abbey's corn came from the Barnhorn estate where early in the 12th century the abbey built what might have been a tide-mill on the marsh to grind the corn into flour.

DEVELOPMENT OF BATTLE TOWN

The needs of the abbey community led directly to the establishment and growth of the town of Battle, the centre of which today retains much of its original medieval plan. Rental accounts show that by the first years of the 12th century, the majority of the 109 households were English, although a significant minority were incomers from Normandy, while others had intermarried between the two communities. Although Battle gradually developed as a market town, its fortunes and those of the abbey were closely linked. This local relationship was apparent in 1175 when both townspeople and monks crowded into the chapter house to welcome the new abbot Odo, and to hear his first sermon. Many sons of Battle became monks while others ran its secular affairs, and local traders, lawyers, craftsmen and producers of luxury items, such as goldsmiths and silversmiths, depended heavily on its patronage. In later years the abbey also relied on more distant suppliers: an apothecary and a dried-fish merchant in London and a wine importer in Winchelsea. Fourteenth-century records suggest that the abbey spent the substantial sum of between £600 and £650 annually in the town and *leuga*. In about 1300, the town's population was between 2,000 and 3,000 — the same as in the 1930s — making it by far the largest in eastern Sussex. The Black Death in 1348–9, however, probably more than halved the population and led to a reduction in the number of houses over a long period of time. Crucially, though, the abbey provided steady support, not least in the employment given by its various rebuilding campaigns.

The Monks' Day

A monk's daily routine was regulated by a timetable of religious services. Typically, the first service very early in the morning when it was still dark was Nocturns, followed by Matins around dawn. A third service was held before the monks went to the cloister to read for several hours. At about 8am they went back to the dormitory, washed, changed out of their soft leather night boots into their day shoes and returned to the church for the services of Tierce and Mass. They then gathered in the chapter house for the daily reading of a chapter of the Rule of St Benedict. The abbot or prior announced special duties and the daily business of the abbey was discussed. From then until noon they read or worked, before returning to the church for the services of Sext, High Mass and None. At about 2pm the monks went to the refectory for the only substantial meal of the day, followed by more work and reading. Just before sunset they returned to the church for Vespers and then to the refectory for a drink of weak beer, cider, wine or water. The last service of the day was Compline at about 7pm, after which the monks retired to bed in the dormitory.

The monks assembled in the chapter house for the daily reading of a chapter of the Rule of St Benedict

Above: A Benedictine monk writing in this illustration from a 12th-century book of psalms. Copying manuscripts in the scriptorium was an important part of the monks' daily work

Left: Benedictine monks celebrating an elaborate mass from a 15th-century French manuscript. On the left monks sing from a communal song book, while on the right, a priest at the altar leads the service

Right: The great gatehouse, with its battlements, arrow slits and strong gateway, was built at the start of the Hundred Years War in the 1330s. It could have successfully resisted French raiding parties

WAR, PLAGUE AND RECOVERY

The outbreak of the Hundred Years War in the 1330s affected the abbey profoundly as settlements all along the south coast of England fell victim to French raids. The abbot of Battle, as a major landowner, was the chief organizer of coastal defence between Romney Marsh and the Pevensey Levels. In 1338, Abbot Alan de Retlyng (1324–50) mustered all available men to guard the port of Winchelsea, which was an embarkation point for soldiers heading to France. The same year, he began to strengthen Battle Abbey's precinct wall, parts of which still exist, and to build the present gatehouse with its defensive features. These were not just for protection against French raids. As the war progressed, there was growing unrest and lawlessness in the region. In 1354 Abbot Robert de Bello (1351–64) complained that it was almost impossible to reach the abbey's remote manor of Dengemarsh on Romney Marsh because of the hostility of local men to visitors. As French raids worsened, the abbey almoner provided food and clothing for poor refugees fleeing inland. In the summer of 1377 Hastings was sacked. In the same year the French also raided Winchelsea, and Abbot Hamo of Battle (1364–83) gained lasting fame when he led his forces in the successful defence of the town. The abbey records mention this warrior-abbot's hauberk (coat of mail) and crossbow; in more peaceful times, he probably used his crossbow on the hunting field.

In the middle of these troubles came the Black Death of 1348–9. The population of the town was probably halved, while the monastic community was reduced from 52 to 34 by 1352. This loss of population affected the abbey's rental income and the profitability of its agricultural estates. Bubonic plague returned at intervals, although on only one occassion did it have the same devastating effects on the abbey as the Black Death. Battle was fortunate to have a number of capable abbots who managed its estates carefully and avoided serious debt despite the falling income. Their strong local connections – three were born in Battle – undoubtedly helped the town and abbey to avoid the more serious unrest that culminated in the Peasants' Revolt of 1381. However, by the early 15th century, the number of monks had fallen to 23.

The last century of the abbey's existence was a period of comparative tranquillity. Visiting churchmen reported that religious observances were being maintained and by 1490 the numbers of monks had grown to 31, including the prior. The abbey's revenues also appear to have revived, allowing the abbot to make extensive alterations and additions to his house in the west range and to reconstruct the cloister walks with handsome new traceried windows and vaulting. The small fireplaces installed in the dormitory probably also date from this time.

THE SUPPRESSION

In 1529 John Hamond was elected the 30th abbot of Battle. He was to be the last. He came from a local country family long associated with the abbey and had risen to be the sacristan (the monk who took care of the church fabric and its contents), before being appointed head of the house. By then there were growing signs that monastic life was under serious threat from the state. The ostensible reasons were that monastic religious observances were felt to be moribund and the monks guilty of all sorts of crimes; the reality was that King Henry VIII (1509–47) and his advisers such as Thomas Cromwell (d.1540) wanted monastic lands and assets.

In the summer of 1535 Battle Abbey was inspected by Thomas Cromwell's notorious visitor, Dr Richard Layton (d.1544), who unjustly described Hamond as 'the veriest hayne, beetle

and buserde and the arentest chorle that ever I see' ['the meanest wretch, numb-skull and dim-wit, and the most out-and-out bumpkin I ever met']. In May 1538, Layton returned to Battle to make an inventory of the contents, and when this was completed on 27 May, Hamond and 18 monks surrendered the house. Although Layton described Battle as 'so beggary a house I never see, nor so filthy stuff', its income of £880 in 1535 made it one of the more prosperous Benedictine houses. The poor state of its furnishings may have been the result of the community anticipating the end and quietly disposing of some of its movable assets. Abbot Hamond was given a substantial annual pension of £100 and moved to a house on the opposite side of Battle High Street, where he died in 1546.

Above: Soldiers looting a house in a late 14th-century French manuscript; such scenes must have accompanied French raids on the English coast during the Hundred Years War, from 1337 to 1453

Left: Lawrence Champion, abbot of Battle 1508–29 (centre), with other abbots and priors at the opening of King Henry VIII's second Parliament in 1512. By the time of his death he would have been aware of the growing threats to monastic life from the State

THE SOUTH-WEST VIEW OF BATTEL-ABBY, IN THE COUNTY OF SUSSEX.

Top: Battle Abbey in 1737, showing the vanished precinct wall between the gatehouse on the left and the 16th-century guest range on the right

Above: A portrait of Sir Anthony Browne who owned the abbey after 1538

Right: The effigy of Sir Anthony Browne from the tomb he shares with his wife Alice, in Battle parish church

BATTLE ABBEY AS A COUNTRY ESTATE

In August 1538, Henry VIII gave Battle Abbey and many of its lands to his close friend and master of the horse, Sir Anthony Browne. Sir Anthony retained the great gatehouse as the formal entrance, but demolished the church, chapter house, refectory and cloister walk and took over the abbot's lodgings as his residence. He, or possibly his son, remodelled the adjacent monastic guest house. Sir Anthony did well from the suppression of monastic communities, at one time owning Bayham and Waverley Abbeys, Easebourne Priory and the Priory of St Mary Overy in Southwark. On his death in 1548 he was buried in Battle church where his effigy lies alongside that of his first wife on a magnificent tomb chest.

Sir Anthony's eldest son was created the first Viscount Montague by Queen Mary. Before his death in 1592 he built the surviving town courthouse, east of the great gatehouse. This was the last significant addition made by the Montagues at Battle Abbey. The family preferred their other residences and seem only occasionally to have visited Battle. In 1685 the fourth viscount demolished the monastic kitchen and sold the materials, and by then the abbot's hall was apparently being used as a barn.

BATTLE ABBEY AND THE WEBSTERS

In 1721 the sixth viscount sold the 3,200ha (8,000 acre) Battle Abbey estate to Sir Thomas Webster for £56,000; it remained with his descendants for most of the next 250 years. Sir Thomas, created a baronet by Queen Anne in 1703, was a rich city merchant, a supplier of hemp to the Royal Navy, and for a number of years a member of parliament. The historical association of Battle Abbey with the Norman Conquest

might have prompted his purchase, for he had a keen interest in history and antiquities. Sir Thomas repaired the former abbot's house and rented out much of the land. He was interested in agriculture, acquiring additional land, and in 1731 buying implements from Jethro Tull, the inventor of the seed drill.

Sir Thomas died in 1751. The following year Horace Walpole visited Battle Abbey and commented favourably on most of the buildings: 'The situation is noble, above the level of abbeys: what does remain of gateways and towers is beautiful.' He was less complimentary about their surroundings: 'The grounds and what has been the park, lie in a vile condition.' This was probably due to a shortage of money, for although Sir Thomas had been rich, the expenses of his estates and businesses were a constant strain on his resources.

Sir Whistler Webster, the second baronet, was also a member of parliament, and lived the life of a country gentleman, managing his estates. Although he seems to have maintained the abbot's house, the rest of the former monastic buildings were neglected. Sir Whistler demolished the monastic guest house except for the two surviving western towers and the undercrofts, as well as pulling down most of the precinct wall along the western boundary of the former outer court. Two years later, at the age of 58, he married Martha Nairn, the 37-year-old daughter of the

Left: A portrait of Sir Whistler Webster, second baronet, 1709–79, responsible for the destruction of several of the abbey buildings in the later 18th century

Below: The abbot's range from the west in 1783 by Samuel Grimm. It shows the general neglect of the abbey buildings and the destruction of the guest range. Only the two 16th-century corner towers of the range seen in the engraving opposite remain. The ivy-covered building to the right of the abbot's hall was rebuilt in 1858 as the library wing

dean of Battle. They had no children and on his death in September 1779 the estate and the baronetcy passed to his younger brother, Sir Godfrey. Sir Godfrey had little time to enjoy his inheritance, dying the following March. The estate passed in turn to his son.

The fourth baronet, another Sir Godfrey, brought disaster upon the estate and the family. He was a captain in the Sussex militia, and a notorious rake and gambler with a famously hot

temper. To fund his gambling and profligate life, he sold outlying parts of the estate. In 1786 he married a 15-year-old heiress, Elizabeth Vassall, and although they had a son in 1789, the marriage was not a success. An extended grand tour of Europe in the 1790s saw Lady Webster with a string of lovers. In 1795 the death of her father left her an annual income of £10,000, together with a West Indian estate for Sir Godfrey that produced a further £7,000 a year, provided he changed his name to Vassall. In 1796, Lady Webster returned from Florence pregnant with Lord Holland's child, and in the following year she and Sir Godfrey divorced. As well as custody of his children, the settlement awarded Sir Godfrey the whole of his wife's fortune during their joint lives, except for an annual maintenance payment to her of £800. He had a further £6,000 from Lord Holland. Three years later, in June 1800, after running up huge gambling debts, Sir Godfrey shot himself in London.

The fifth baronet, Godfrey Vassall Webster, inherited Battle Abbey when he came of age in 1810. A compulsive gambler, he was described by one contemporary as 'one of the greatest blackguards [scoundrels] in London … I never remember … anybody more generally disliked, or more completely excluded from the pale of good company'. After serving in Wellington's army in Spain, in 1812 he returned to Battle where his

great aunt, Martha Webster, who had refused to move out of the abbey, had finally died on Christmas Day 1810. In her 31-year residence, little had been spent on the buildings, which were then nearly derelict. In 1794, the roof of the courthouse had collapsed in a storm. In the abbot's house, so much rain came though the roof that the old woman had been forced to wear wooden clogs to keep her feet dry.

Sir Godfrey threw himself into the task of restoring the estate. The abbot's house was renovated and a new roof provided for the great hall. A new kitchen and service wing were constructed, together with stables, after it proved impracticable to keep horses in the dormitory. An octagonal thatched dairy was built in the fashionable Gothic style in about 1818. Next to it, and probably contemporary, is a substantial ice house. Gardens were laid out and a new pond was dug in the valley. This might have helped to supply water to the 19th-century gunpowder works but its primary purpose was probably to supply ice to the ice house.

After discovering the east end of the abbey church, Sir Godfrey had it excavated. He also commissioned the enormous painting of the battle of Hastings which hangs at the end of the great hall. This was executed by Frank Wilkin (1791–1842), better known as a painter of miniatures, and allegedly depicts Sir Godfrey as

Below: The Battle of Hastings *by Frank Wilkin (1791–1842). A crowned William on horseback salutes the body of King Harold. This painting was recently restored and returned to the great hall, the location for which it was originally intended*

Facing page, top: The duchess of Cleveland in the 1840s. A bridesmaid to Queen Victoria and a train-bearer at her coronation, she was described as, 'without exception the loveliest girl of many a London season'

Facing page, bottom: The fourth duke of Cleveland, Harry Vane, by Frederick Sargent (d.1899)

William the Conqueror finding the dead Harold on the battlefield. The painting probably dates from soon after 1815, perhaps commissioned in the patriotic euphoria following Wellington's victory at Waterloo. Costs involved in repairing the abbey buildings, gambling losses and election expenses led to mounting debts. In 1820 Sir Godfrey resigned as a member of parliament and fled to France to escape his creditors. The estate was placed in the hands of trustees, outlying parts were sold, trees in the park were felled for cash and the abbey was rented out.

In 1836 Sir Godfrey died in London, still in debt and pursued by creditors. The sixth baronet, another Sir Godfrey, and the seventh, Sir Augustus, who succeeded his elder brother when the latter died childless in 1853, both made their careers in the Royal Navy. Sir Augustus found the estate still heavily in debt and like his father had to go abroad to escape his creditors. In 1857, he reluctantly put the whole estate up for sale. By then, only 800ha (2,000 acres) remained from the original 4,000ha (10,000 acres).

LATER 19TH AND 20TH CENTURIES

The new owners were Lord Harry Vane and his wife, soon to be the fourth duke and duchess of Cleveland. They poured money into the estate, modernized and refurnished the abbot's house, added the library wing and in 1876 replaced the windows in the great hall. The gardens and parkland were similarly transformed and under their ownership Battle Abbey enjoyed something of a revival as a private family residence. Their connections led to a constant stream of distinguished guests, including Benjamin Disraeli, H M Stanley, the African explorer who found Dr Livingstone, Lord Kitchener and General Sir Redvers Buller, later famous for the relief of Ladysmith in the Boer War.

After the completion of the Tunbridge Wells to Hastings railway line in 1852, what had long been a trickle of visitors grew into crowds. The abbey grounds were opened on a regular basis. In addition to problems with litter, visitors had no respect for privacy: the duchess recorded that on one occasion crowds peered through the windows into the duke's study, 'where the poor duke sat writing his letters, till they fairly stared him out of countenance, and drove him from the room'. The Clevelands' attempts to control visitors were not always appreciated either. An 1875 guidebook to Sussex remarked, 'Surely a place like this might be left for Englishmen to examine

Remembering the 1931 Fire

Mrs Rhona Noel-Clarke (née Higinbotham) was at school at the abbey and remembers the fire on the night of 31 January 1931, when she was 15:

'We had always been told that if the big bell in the abbot's hall tolled, it was a real fire, not a practice. I remember waking up and hearing the bell toll and knowing it was a fire. We had the most excellent fire drill which was always being rehearsed, so we didn't panic. We knew exactly what to do.

'I was supposed to go up the stairs by my dormitory and fetch down a dormitory of younger ones. But when I tried to get up those stairs, I couldn't because of the flames – I could see them coming through the boards. As soon as I could find someone, I told them that I simply couldn't get up the stairs. They said not to worry, because someone from up there had brought them down another way.

'As we came out of our dormitory, on the left were all our best clothes on a rail. None of us thought to take them with us. I lost all my decent clothes except for the garden things that were in the cloakroom – the old coats and the wellington boots and so on.

'We went out onto the drive. I do remember standing and seeing the whole thing alight. It was really horrific. We were all taken down into the gateway where the gym was. We spent the rest of the night on the floor. Afterwards, the town of Battle was wonderfully kind to us and a lot of us were boarded out for the rest of the term. I slept in the deanery as a guest of the dean and his wife.'

'When I tried to get up those stairs, I couldn't because of the flames – I could see them coming through the boards'

Above: Rhona Higinbotham (centre) in a school photograph of 1931 taken at Bolney Court in West Sussex, where the school temporarily relocated while the abbey buildings were reconstructed
Below: The abbot's range in flames on the night of the fire

unshackled by half a score of absurd conditions and free from the constant supervision of a greedy janitor, whose cry, like the horse-leech's daughter is – "Give! Give!"'

The duke of Cleveland died in 1891, followed ten years later by his widow, and once again Battle Abbey was put up for sale. To considerable local enthusiasm, the purchaser was Sir Augustus Webster, the eighth baronet. Buying back the estate was the fulfilment of a family dream, but it came at a cost. Although Sir Augustus had married Mabel Crossley, the sole heiress of the Crossley carpet company fortune, he still had to fund almost the entire purchase in a series of mortgages. He and his wife lived at Powdermill House on the estate and rented out the abbey. Tragically, in June 1917 Mabel drowned while swimming in a local pond; two months later their only son Godfrey was killed in the third battle of Ypres.

In 1923, Sir Augustus Webster died and the estate was placed in the hands of trustees for the benefit of his two daughters. In 1922, the abbey buildings were leased to the school that still occupies the site. On the night of 31 January 1931, a fire swept through most of the buildings, causing serious damage. They were carefully restored by the architect and antiquary Sir Harold Brakespear, who also excavated part of the cloister.

After the fall of France in June 1940, the War Office commandeered Battle Abbey for army accommodation. During the war, units of the Royal Artillery, the Somerset Light Infantry and others were based here. Temporary camps and

Above: Lady Mabel Webster, wife of Sir Augustus Webster, eighth baronet, with their son Godfrey (standing) and baby daughter Lucy, from The Tatler, *11 December 1901*
Right: The visitor centre at Battle Abbey, which was completed in 2007, explores the background and events of the battle of Hastings, 1066
Below: Girls at school in the abbey in the 1920s. Webster family portraits decorate the walls

vehicle parks were laid out in the grounds. From late summer 1941, the abbey was mostly occupied by the Canadian 1st Army, responsible for the defence of the Sussex coast. In 1942, many of these soldiers were killed in the disastrous Dieppe raid. Two years later, on D-Day (6 June 1944), troops from Battle took part in the invasion of Normandy. For these men, history had come full circle almost 900 years after Duke William's forces sailed from Normandy to the battle of Hastings.

On 3 February 1943, Battle Abbey gatehouse had a narrow escape when German bombs fell on the High Street. One bomb hit the ground just outside the gatehouse, ricocheted past a sentry, knocking his rifle from his hand, then went through the gate-passage, damaging one of the gates and the adjacent pier. It hit the porter's doorway and the western pedestrian archway, before breaking up on the lawn without exploding. The repairs to the porter's doorway can still be seen.

In 1976, the Webster trustees finally put the Battle Abbey estate up for sale. The government bought it with the aid of donations by a group of Americans wishing to commemorate the bicentenary of American independence. It is now in the care of English Heritage and over the past 30 years much work has been done to conserve the historic buildings and the estate. In 2007, an exhibition exploring the battle of Hastings was completed at the abbey, reminding visitors of the enduring significance of the events that happened here over 900 years ago.